Ant and Grasshopper

by Catherine Baker
illustrated by Davide Ortu

One August day, Grasshopper was in the meadow. He was feasting on the juice of fallen apples.

"Life is sweet!" he said. "I can just enjoy myself. There's no need to work."

Grasshopper was right. He never had to feel hungry. There was delicious food all around him.

The sun shone every day. Grasshopper was very pleased with his life.

Grasshopper made up a merry song. The music came from his back legs. They rubbed over his wings, making a buzzing noise.

Suddenly, Grasshopper spotted something in the grass nearby. It was an ant! She was struggling to carry a heavy wheat grain. Grasshopper gawped at her curiously.

As Grasshopper watched, Ant struggled on. She carried the grain to her nest. Then she went back for another grain. She did this time and time again!

“That looks far too challenging!” said Grasshopper.

Finally, Ant stopped. She was trying to drag a whole corn cob. It was far too big for her.

"I've had enough!" she said. "Please help me carry this corn, Grasshopper."

However, Grasshopper had no intention of helping Ant. He shook his head lazily. He laid back among the colourful flowers.

Then he sang a song.

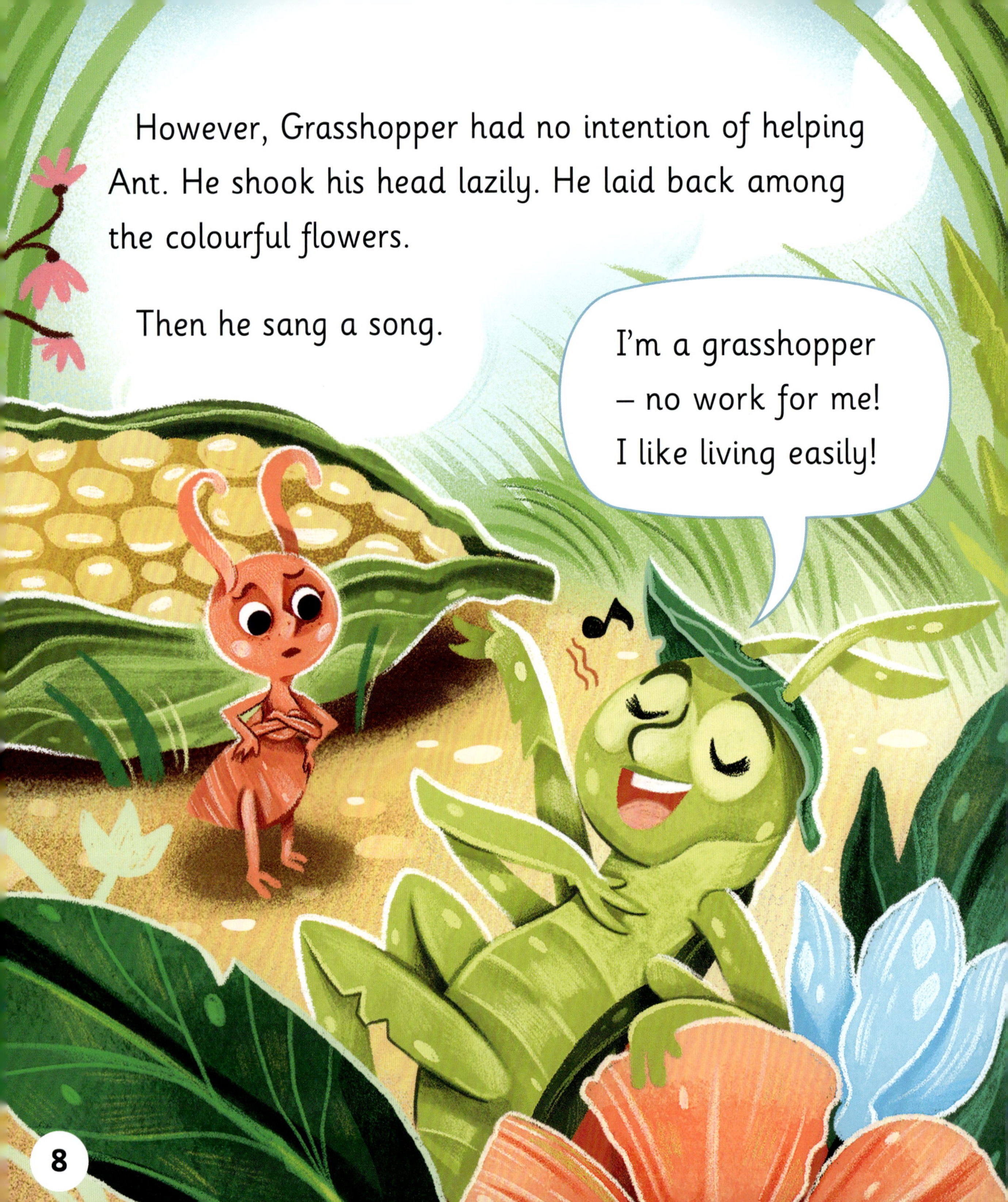

"Very well," said Ant, crossly. "You'll be sorry in the winter. Then all your food will be gone. However, my nest will be full of food. You'll have nothing."

"The winter's ages off," grinned Grasshopper. "It's silly to worry about that!"

Ant just shook her head sadly. Grasshopper watched her struggle off to her nest. She was still heaving the huge corn cob.

Grasshopper shrugged and whistled a little tune to himself. Then he started munching the luscious grass again. He soon forgot all about Ant.

"This is the life!" he said, cheerfully.

When September came, the weather turned cooler. Soon, chilly breezes began to blow.

Yet Grasshopper still found plenty of food. He continued to do nothing but eat, sing and rest.

One October day, Grasshopper saw Ant and her sisters. They were carrying some big, ripe berries.

"We're heading back to the nest," said Ant. "Be on your guard, Grasshopper – winter's coming!"

However, Grasshopper took no notice.

The cold days arrived. Grasshopper could find less and less food. Still, he sang as loudly as he could. He wanted to show he was brave.

However, Grasshopper knew life was getting tougher. He just didn't want to admit his real feelings. The truth was, he was getting a bit worried.

One day, the first snow fell. Grasshopper's field was cold and glistening white. Grasshopper looked at the ghastly scene around him. There was no food left at all. What a shock!

Now, Grasshopper couldn't even make music. He had a nasty cough. Both his wings were frozen stiff. His legs were creaky with cold, too.

"What am I going to do?" he wondered.

“I know!” croaked Grasshopper. “I’ll go and visit Ant. There’s plenty of food in her nest. She told me so herself.”

So Grasshopper creaked over to Ant’s nest.

Grasshopper peered into the nest. There was Ant, snug and cosy. She was playing games with her sisters. It looked like a lot of fun.

Grasshopper, frozen and hungry, felt sorry for himself.

“Please may I have some food?” Grasshopper begged. He began singing a tiny, creaky song.

However, Ant shook her head.

"Why should we help you?" she asked. "When I was struggling, you refused to help me. You even called me silly. I was only planning ahead for the winter!"

"I'm sorry," said Grasshopper. "I see now that I was wrong."

He turned slowly away and began to trudge back. He hobbled across the wintry field.

Suddenly, Ant took pity on the dejected grasshopper.

"Hold on!" Ant called out to Grasshopper. She handed him a bag of corn. "I hope you've learned your lesson!" she added.

"Yes!" sang Grasshopper, gratefully.

Grasshopper's Feelings

How is Grasshopper feeling at each of these points in the story? Why is he feeling like that?

Encourage students to look at the pictures and talk about Grasshopper's feelings in each one.